As It Is

As It Is

The Open Secret to
Living an Awakened Life

Tony Parsons

InnerDirections
P U B L I S H I N G

InnerDirections Publishing

INNER DIRECTIONS FOUNDATION
P.O. Box 130070
Carlsbad, California 92013
Phone: (800) 545-9118
www.InnerDirections.org

First North American Edition
Printed in Canada on recycled paper

Book & cover design by Joan Greenblatt

ISBN: 1-878019-10-4
Library of Congress Catalog Card Number: 00-105744

The publisher gratefully acknowledges
the kind help of *The Ward Foundation*,
Box 2137, Friday Harbor, WA 98250
in sponsoring the publication of this book.

The nature of liberation is direct, simple, and as natural as breathing. Many will come across it and shuffle quickly back to that which they think they can know and do. But there are those with whom the invitation will resonate . . . they will suddenly see and be ready to let go of all seeking, even for that which they have called enlightenment.

CONTENTS

FOREWORD

One hint that you are in the presence of an awakened one is that however hard you try to catch hold of them or their teaching, you always come away empty-handed. This is the open secret of their awakened presence. Though teachings on awakening cannot be fully grasped by the mind, the immediacy of authentic understanding is always available to the heart that is open.

And so it was my delight that, after spending an afternoon in conversation with Tony Parsons, I walked away empty-handed. What did linger, however, was the resonance of who and what Tony Parsons is.

Tony lives comfortably in the paradoxical understanding that there is neither "separate self" nor "independent other," and affirms this through his words and his presence. In these simple teachings, we find the way to be born anew and experience the timeless wisdom based on the nondual teachings of Oneness.

In Tony's company, I found neither a teacher nor a preacher but a presence which allowed our conversation to unfold and blossom in a palpable silence that was rooted in the present moment. With eyes that twinkle and an infectious ease of being, Tony uses no complex jargon when communicating with others. His words are simple yet uncompromisingly clear and come directly from the immediacy of his own experience. In his presence you know that he is not identified with his " . . . life story, the mind, the body, experiences of pain or pleasure, success or failure, stillness, compassion, seeking, finding, or anything which is called a spiritual experience."

What you do find in Tony is a presence, which allows everything to be "as it is." And he is emphatic that ". . . nothing, absolutely nothing, needs to be added or taken away from ourselves in order to be who we are. No conditions need to be fulfilled. The infinite is not somewhere else waiting for us to become worthy." Tony's words are both descriptive and prescriptive: let life be, just as it is.

What you won't find in *As It Is* are techniques or processes that will bring us to this understanding of Oneness. Though this may frustrate some readers, Tony is adamantly steadfast in his revelation that the only way to realize our true nature is to be with life "as it is," without trying to change anything. After all, since there is no separate self, "who" is to affect change? When we take life on its own terms, as Tony affirms through his own experience, everything will be discovered to be ". . . the ground of unconditional love, for there is nothing that is not sacred, and, regardless of any particular state I might be in, I see that grace is continuously available. Look, here is the secret (picks up a sweater and throws it on the floor). In the dream, we see a separate object. When there is no illusory, separate self, the ground of un-conditional love is seen. This is what is always open and available to us. There is nothing that exists outside of the ground of this natural unity. The 'secret' is that there is no separation, but it remains a secret as long as we believe we are 'someone.'"

Tony's book, *As It Is*, is a jewel of simplicity with a timeless message for the heart that is ready to realize that "There is no need to wait for transformation, to look for the nondoer, permanent bliss, an egoless state, or a still mind. You don't even have to wait for grace to descend, for you are, I am, it is already the abiding grace."

And the grace is that this book is now in your hands.

Richard C. Miller, Ph.D.
Sebastopol, California
June 2000

INTRODUCTION

This is a book declaring that enlightenment is a sudden, direct, and energetic illumination that is continuously available to anyone who is ready to let go and allow it. It is the open secret, which reveals itself in every part of our lives. No effort, path of purification, process, or teaching of any kind can take us there, for the open secret is not about our effort to change the way we live—it is about the rediscovery of "who" it is that lives.

No one concept, or set of concepts, can express enlightenment. To attempt to share through words the rediscovery and wonder of who we are is as futile a process as writing a recipe for plum pudding and expecting someone reading it to be able to taste it.

It seems to me that verbal communication can only be an expression of an understanding, and I am sharing my understanding of what I feel is the most significant and liberating insight that is possible to comprehend.

There is nothing new that is being expressed here. We all have a sense of this illumination, which has been written and spoken about in various ways and from differing influences and backgrounds.

Some people I have shared this with have carefully labeled it and filed it away. Many have come across it and quickly shuffled back to that which they think they can "know" and "do." Others have said that "life is not that simple." I have to say that simplicity was one of the most wonderful qualities that surprised me about this revelation, together with its all-encompassing nature. There are those who believe that "enlightenment takes time" or that they need to experience various processes or realize certain beliefs before considering "this kind of approach." Some have complained that they have used present awareness and "nothing has changed or improved"! Others vigorously reject the idea that freedom can be realized in any other way than through effort, sacrifice, and discipline. And some have heard this message and made the leap in their own unique way.

But from wherever and whenever this insight is communicated, it has no connection with end-gaining, belief, path, or process. It cannot be taught but is continuously shared. Because it is our inheritance, no one can lay claim to it. It needs not to be argued, proven, or embellished, for it stands alone simply as it is, and can only remain unrecognized and rejected, or realized and lived.

Part 1
REFLECTIONS

AWAKENING
FROM THE
DREAM

While we remain locked within the apparent experience of being separate individuals living in an existence with which we have to negotiate, we live in a state of dreaming.

In that dream state, all that we do is governed by the law of opposites in which every so-called positive act is exactly and equally balanced by its opposite.

Therefore, all of our individual attempts to make our lives work, to reach perfection or to attain personal liberation, are neutralized.

We discover, through deep reflection and understanding, that as long as we continue in this dream we are, in reality, living in a circle. We are on a wheel on which everything is continually repeating itself over and over again in differing images. It is consciousness delighting in a creation that is both constrained and liberated. And despite what we believe about our individuality and free will, we come to see that we are only dreamed characters reacting and responding from a set of conditioned and historical belief systems.

All of classic religion, art, and science in a world that we see as progressive comes within the parameters of this perfectly balanced and exactly neutral state, which serves only to reflect another possibility. In terms of actual liberation, nothing is happening. What we have apparently created is apparently destroyed. And what we have apparently destroyed is apparently recreated.

Moving from our original and timeless nature into consciousness identified, we have created this circumstance in order to rediscover that the dream we are living has absolutely no purpose other than our awakening from it. That awakening emerges outside of the dream, outside of time, and is completely beyond the grasp of individual effort, path, process, or belief.

CONTEXT

When I was very young, I had a sense of being in a magic world, outside of time. There was no need to have to become something or do anything—just an unrecognized oneness that enveloped me simply in the wonder of "what is." I feel it is the same for most children.

One day, all of that changed and I entered the world of separation and need. I found that I had a separate mother and father, a name, and an apparent choice to do this or that. I moved into the world of time and space, boundary and exploration, endeavor, manipulation, and the pursuit of pleasure and avoidance of pain.

I came to own these experiences and believed they were my natural way of being.

I was also taught and came to believe that if I worked hard, behaved myself and succeeded in my chosen or imposed job, got married, had children and looked after my health, I stood a good chance of being happy. I did all of this quite successfully and enjoyed myself at times, but I also recognized that something intangible and fundamental seemed to be missing. A secret of some kind.

Consequently, I decided to seek out what was missing through religion.

Again, I was told that if I worked hard and applied

myself to various disciplines, rituals, and purifications, I would eventually come to deserve "spiritual fulfillment." Again, I completely involved myself in whatever seemed appropriate, but still could not discover the reason for my sense of longing.

One day, almost as if by accident, I rediscovered the secret that I had known as a small child; or perhaps it rediscovered me.

To explain what happened is quite impossible. The description that comes nearest to it is that of being overwhelmed with a love and a total comprehension that is absolutely beyond imagination.

The revelation that accompanied this rediscovery was so simple and yet so revolutionary that it swept away in a stroke all that I had been taught or had come to believe.

Part of that realization was that enlightenment is absolutely beyond my effort to change the way I live, or even of changing life at all. It has to do with a total shift in the realization of "who" it is that lives.

For I am already that which I seek. Whatever I seek or think I want, however long the shopping list may be, all of my desires are only a reflection of my longing to come home. And home is oneness; home is my original nature. It is right here, simply in "what is." There is nowhere else I have to go, and nothing else I have to become.

Since that time I have embraced and lived that

revelation—and avoided and rejected it.

It is, of course, impossible to communicate in words the inexpressible, and so this declaration is my attempt to express my understanding of that revelation. I try to explain the way in which my beliefs about enlightenment, time, purpose, and my effort to achieve spiritual fulfillment can directly interrupt that oneness that is continuously and directly available, how the illusion of separation, fear, guilt and abstraction can distract me from the freedom that includes and transforms these influences.

I also express in the best way I can how effortless and natural it is to let go and be open to that freedom.

To see this work as an exhortation to lead a meditative life or to "be here now" would be to miss the point entirely.

This declaration speaks about a singular and revolutionary leap in perception about what we really are. It requires no embellishment or lengthy explanation and, once realized, leaves nothing more to be said.

For the sake of clarity, the terms *enlightenment, liberation, fulfillment, freedom, oneness,* and so on, are all seen here as being the same as the absolute realization by anyone of what they really are.

As It Is

No
Achievement

For me, the first realization of enlightenment, or of the nature of who I really am, is not something that can be expressed. What happened cannot even be called an experience, because the separate experiencer needed to be absent for it to emerge.

However, what accompanied that happening was a realization of such simple magnitude and revolutionary content that it left me awestruck and quite alone.

One of the things I came to see is that enlightenment only becomes available when it has been accepted that it cannot be achieved.

Doctrines, processes, and progressive paths that seek enlightenment only exacerbate the problem they address by reinforcing the idea that the self can find something that it presumes it has lost. It is that very effort, that investment in self-identity that continuously recreates the illusion of separation from oneness. This is the veil that we believe exists. It is the dream of individuality.

It is like someone who imagines that they are in a deep hole in the earth, and in order to escape they dig deeper and deeper, throwing the earth behind them and covering up the light that is already there.

The only likely effect of extreme effort to become "that which I already am," is that eventually I will drop to the ground, exhausted, and let go. In that letting go, another possibility may arise. But the temptation to avoid freedom through the sanctification of struggle is very attractive. Struggle in time does not invite liberation.

Life is not a task. There is absolutely nothing to attain except the realization that there is absolutely nothing to attain.

No amount of effort will ever persuade oneness to appear. All that is needed is a leap in perception, a different seeing, already inherent but unrecognized.

As It Is

NO ONE
BECOMES
ENLIGHTENED

I used to believe that people actually became enlight-ened, and that the event was similar to someone winning the jackpot in a national lottery. Once the prize had been won, the beneficiary would thereafter be guaranteed permanent bliss, infallibility, and incorrupt-ible goodness.

In my ignorance, I thought these people had obtained and owned something that made them special and totally different from me. This illusory idea reinforced in me the belief that enlightenment was virtually unobtain-able except for an extraordinary and chosen few. These misconceptions sprang from some image I held of how a state of perfection should look. I was not yet able to see that enlightenment has nothing to do with the idea of perfection. These beliefs were greatly strengthened when I compared my imagined inadequacies with the picture I held of whichever "spiritual hero" I happened to be attracted to at the time.

I feel that most people see enlightenment in a similar way.

Certainly there have been, and still are, many who seek to encourage such beliefs and who have actually claimed to have become enlightened. I now see that this is as pointless a declaration as someone proclaiming to the world that they can breathe.

Essentially the realization of enlightenment brings with it the sudden comprehension that there is no one and nothing to be enlightened. Enlightenment simply is. It cannot be owned, just as it cannot be achieved or won like some trophy. All and everything is oneness, and all that we do gets in its way by trying to find it.

Those who make claims of enlightenment or take certain stances have simply not realized its paradoxical nature and presume ownership of a state they imagine they have achieved. They are likely to have had a deep personal experience of some kind, but this bears absolutely no relationship to illumination. Consequently, they still remain locked in their own individual concepts based on their own particular belief systems.

These people often need to take on the role of "spiritual teachers" or "enlightened masters" and inevitably attract those who need to be students or disciples. Their teaching, still rooted in dualism, inevitably promotes a schism between the "teacher" and those who choose to follow the teaching. As the following increases, so does the exclusive role of the master need to be enhanced.

One of the usual symptoms, when such a role has been adopted, is a clampdown of any admission or sign of "human weakness." This condition usually creates distance between the "master" and his or her followers.

As the specialness of the "master" becomes more

effective, and the demands of the followers become greater, so invariably do the teachings become more obscure and convoluted. As the obscurity of the teaching increases, so does the schism get wider, and many of the followers often become more confused and submissive. The usual effect on those involved can be unquestioning adulation, disillusionment, or an awakening and moving on.

However, these kinds of influences have established and maintained an illusory sense of doubt and inadequacy in the collective unconscious about people's ability to open to and realize something that is as natural, simple, and available as breathing.

Those who have fully comprehended and embraced enlightenment have absolutely nothing to sell. When they share their understanding, they have no need to embellish themselves or what they share. Neither do they have any interest in being mothers, fathers, or teachers.

Exclusivity breeds exclusion, but freedom is shared through friendship.

TIME

In my condition of separation I came to accept, without question, the existence and effect of time. Together with my belief in time, I was inevitably married to the concept and experience of a beginning, a middle, and an end—a journey towards the realization of a goal or conclusion.

This concept of a journey can be applied at any level, whether it is doing well at school, creating a successful business, or realizing enlightenment. It was all a path to becoming—a reaching out for a result in time.

This message was etched most powerfully into my psyche by what appeared to me to be the process of birth and death. Such a mighty message reflected and reinforced the seeming irrefutability of time's existence, passage, and effect. As I experienced what had appeared to be the effect of time, so did I come to believe in it. As I believed in the existence of time, I also came to believe in the limitation of my own existence. As I came to accept that limitation, I also came to believe that I needed to make use of the period given. I had to do something, achieve something, become something worthwhile during the time that I imagined remained. Consequently, the concept of "purpose" was born, and together with it my expectation and investment in what that purpose might bring.

As It Is

EXPECTATION
& PURPOSE

I became locked into the limitation of time and separation through the expectation I had about purpose. I have been in pursuit of a variety of goals and purposes in my life, including spiritual ones. Within the traditional religious ethic, I came across a kaleidoscope of western and eastern doctrines and concepts, which I believed represented a rich tradition of authoritative wisdom.

As a consequence of what I saw as my spiritual lack, I decided I had to do something—belong to something, become something worthwhile. I had to find a model of reality which would satisfy my need to feel I was making some sort of progress towards some sort of goal.

I decided to try to become a Christian.

Considering the information I had at the time, it seemed that this approach was appropriate. I had my western background, my knowledge of biblical history and tradition, and the apparently unimpeachable truths, processes, and rituals presented to me—original sin, prayer, confession, forgiveness, communion and purification, and the written and spoken word.

I felt I was doing my best with what at the time I understood and sanctified, and what I anticipated and expected would give meaning to my spiritual life. If I tried harder, tomorrow would be better than today, another

As It Is

place would be better than this place.

I came to believe in the message of inadequacy, which leads through repentance to a given grace, through which I would eventually be seen to be "deserving" and would ultimately evolve from a lower to a higher level of existence.

I now had the wherewithal I thought I needed to realize the purpose I believed would fulfill me.

I could solicit with prayer and negotiate through performance, while "God the Father" sat foursquare in heaven and kept the accounts.

It seemed there was so much opportunity, so much knowledge, and so much time in which to give meaning to my life, for it to become something better—something worthy. And my purpose was married to my hope. For it was the hope of better things to come that inspired me to struggle and strive, resist and persist in order to strengthen my sense of direction. I could now make spiritual progress for myself and help others to do the same.

Purpose, hope, and belief gave me the energy and the will to succeed. Purpose, hope and belief—these revered and seemingly powerful values which are acknowledged by many as so worthwhile. But of course they also exist in the shadow of confusion, hopelessness, and despair. At the time, I had not reckoned on that side of things. Eventually and inevitably, the swinging pendulum of endless encounters with expectation and disappointment, effort and inadequacy, apparent strength and weakness all played their part in my awakening from this dream.

All of those communions and confessions, and all of those spiritual tasks seemed endless—that greedy, bottomless, spiritual shopping basket that I would have to fill with prayer, abstinence, humility, worship, and good deeds, and if I ever got to the bottom of that one I would have to fill another, probably beginning with obedience and chastity.

I tried and I tried, but it all seemed so archaic and joyless in some way. The expectation that an already fearsome and inadequate follower could, through the discipline of negation and worship, become anything other than a fearsome and inadequate follower, seemed as futile as the idea of celibacy being a route to celebration and wholeness. I felt as though I was trying to bake a cake without any juice.

It seems to me that any attempt to translate the inexpressible into the doctrinal must inevitably end up as a misrepresentation—a contradictory idea about perfection that transforms the originator's subtle and beautiful song of freedom into an interminable dogma of limitation. When the bird has flown, the essence of its song is often mislaid, and then all we are left with is an empty cage.

I like the story of God and the Devil watching man as he discovered something beautiful in a desert. "*Aha,*" said God to the Devil, "*now that man has found truth you will have nothing to do."* *"On the contrary,"* replied the Devil, *"I am going to help him organize it."*

Whenever or wherever there is organized religion, there also can most easily flourish a rich breeding ground for our worst fears, our darkest guilt, and our ugliest conflicts, person to person, nation to nation, and faith to faith. Whether we hold a religious belief or not, these wounds can lie deep within us and invade every part of our experience.

It felt unnatural and limiting to support an ethic based on such a purgative "no" and carefully considered "yes" when I intuitively recognized that what I was looking for was absolutely beyond both. In these circumstances, I moved on and investigated the world of contemporary therapy and spirituality.

These approaches to fulfillment seemed to me to be so much more intelligent and inclusive than anything I had previously come across; the ideas were so very open and liberating.

It was tremendously exciting to be offered the means whereby I could learn to uncover, heal, and integrate those parts of my life which seemed to interfere with my relationships with people, creativity, health and wealth and, most importantly of all, my own sense of self-worth.

If all of us could do this, what a wonderful world it could become. It appealed to me, especially in contrast to the idea of having to shape myself to a way of life based on someone else's conceptual model of how I should be.

As It Is

There were so many interesting and new processes to choose from, and so many people to share with in what felt like a twentieth-century spiritual adventure. It was fascinating to be involved in shocking and illuminating breakthroughs, the rush of emotions, the fear and excitement of revealing my innermost secrets, of truly surrendering to my guru, of discovering why I was so fascinated by and so frightened of women. Sharing in other people's agonies and revelations, past life memories, present assaults and future hopes and dreads, all was a revelation and a confirmation.

It was all so exciting, and it was all about me!

I involved myself in the deepest and most illuminating meditations, consumed the most recent and significant books, and, of course, threw myself with much enthusiasm into the latest therapies. They burst out of the ground like new fruits to be sucked and digested, or tasted and thrown away—this breathing method, that affirmation, this integration, that special and significant energy—all had a fascination for me in those early days. If these activities were seen to be introspective or self-indulgent, then I had already recognized that, with one exception: all choice is generated from apparent self-motivation.

The expression of feelings became sacrosanct, together with the need to think positively, forgive my mother, heal my inner child, delve into my past, and so on. All of these things became vital and important processes to follow—rather like a modern day "Ten Commandments."

I spent a year doing an intensive residential course experiencing many key contemporary therapies mixed with Eastern meditations. After a while I settled on those therapies or methods I felt suited me and brought me most benefit.

I experienced considerable movement of previously held inhibitions and came to recognize belief systems and patterns that had strongly influenced much of my early behavior.

In most of the "inner work" people do, it appears that the strengthening and reinforcement of a sense of self-identity and self-worth is the primary aim. The theory seems to be that if I can embrace and assimilate these processes, then I can eventually emerge as a more alive, balanced, and effective individual with a clear idea about relationships and my part in the whole. All of that structure would need to be built on a powerful set of belief systems developed from considerable discipline and effort. But belief resides within the shadow of doubt. It only functions effectively in direct proportion to the suppression of the doubt that it seeks to override.

I began to see again that I was trying to repair and put together what I took to be related pieces, hoping they might eventually come together to make a whole. But this approach directly contradicted my understanding that enlightenment lay beyond my efforts and expectations concerning self-identity and self-worth.

For those who seek change as individuals within the wheel of life, the contemporary therapeutic world offers tremendous scope and a much deeper and more accepting approach than anything that has gone before.

In my case, the first realization of enlightenment directly followed my moving on from the religious path when I was about twenty-one years old. A few years after this, I involved myself in the contemporary therapies, thinking that they could be a vehicle for communicating the deeper possibility.

I have experienced that the kind of energy generated in certain therapeutic settings can open people to a deeper perception about the nature of awareness and its implications. But here again, I still found myself occupied and fascinated by my expectations surrounding time, purposes, and goals.

In the world of time, purposes and goals are perfectly appropriate, but there is so much investment placed on the attachment and expectations that surround them— becoming this, belonging to that, processes to change, or to be better, methods to purify, and so on. Important new people and places, masters of consciousness and teachers of truths spring up from everywhere and offer their own particular formula for living. And as we move from one to another we seem unwilling to see that freedom does not reside in one place or another, simply because freedom, by its very nature, cannot be excluded or exclusive.

As It Is

We seem not to see that, as we march towards the next anticipated "spiritual" high, the treasure that we seek is to be discovered not in where we are going, but within the simple nature of the very footsteps that we take. In our rush to find a better situation in time, we trample over the flower of beingness that presents itself in every moment.

It seems to me that our attachment to purpose is born from the need to prove something to ourselves. But life is simply life, and is not trying to prove anything at all. This springtime will not try to be better than last springtime, and neither will an ash tree try to become an oak.

By letting go our fascination with the extraordinary and spectacular, we can allow ourselves to recognize the simple wonder that lies within the ordinary.

For life is its own purpose and doesn't need a reason to be. That is its beauty.

As It Is

THE PARK

One day, I was walking across a park in a suburb of London. I noticed as I walked that my mind was totally occupied with expectations about future events that might or might not happen. I apparently made the choice to let go of these projections and simply be with my walking. I noticed that each footstep was totally unique in feel and pressure, and that it was there one moment and gone the next, never to be repeated in the same way ever again.

As all of this was happening, there was a transition from me watching my walking to simply the presence of walking. What happened then is simply beyond description. I can only inadequately say in words that total stillness and presence seemed to descend over everything. All and everything became timeless and I no longer existed. I vanished and there was no longer an experiencer.

Oneness with all and everything was what happened. I can't say I was "at one" because "I" had disappeared. I can only say that oneness with all and everything as what happened, and an overwhelming love filled everything. Together with this there came a total comprehension of the whole. All of this happened in a timeless flash that seemed eternal.

As It Is

Contained within, and directly following this happening, occurred a revelation so magnificent and revolutionary in its nature that I had to sit down on the grass in order to take in its consequence. What I saw was simple and obvious in one way but completely untranslatable in another. It was as if I had been given an answer that had no question. I had been shown a secret that is an open secret; and that all and everything that is known or unknown contains and reflects this open secret. Nature, people, birth and death, and our struggles, our fears and our desires are all contained within and reflect unconditional love.

I felt I had been suddenly overtaken and everything took on a new sense. I looked at grass, trees, dogs, and people, moving as before, but now I not only recognized their essence but I was their essence, as they were mine. It was in another way as if everything, including me, was enveloped in a deep and all-encompassing love, and in a strange way it seemed that what I saw was also somehow nothing special . . . it is the norm that is not usually perceived.

Why me and why now? How could I have deserved to receive such a gift for nothing in return? I was certainly not pure in the biblical sense, or in any other recognized sense, or so my mind told me. I had not lived a disciplined life of meditation or of spiritual dedication of any kind. This illumination had occurred without any effort on my part! I had simply watched my walking in a very easy and natural way, and then this treasure had emerged.

I also came to recognize that this apparent gift had always been available and always would be. That was the most wonderful realization of all! That utterly regardless of where, when, or how I was, this presence was ready to emerge and embrace me. This treasure was to be rediscovered, though not through arduous and seemingly significant spiritual practices and rituals. Not at all. This wonderful all-encompassing treasure was available within the essence of a footstep, in the sound of a tractor, in my feeling of boredom, in the sitting of a cat, in feelings of pain and rejection, on a mountaintop, or in the middle of Balham High Street. Anywhere and everywhere I am totally surrounded and embraced in stillness, unconditional love and oneness.

Later on I began to wonder how this treasure could be retained. But I have again and again come to see that what I had sought to rediscover can never be achieved or contained. There is nothing I have to do, and the very belief that I have to do anything to deserve this treasure interrupts its inherent quality.

And this is again the paradox, for the divine instinct is continuously available, simply through the allowing of it. It is always at hand, in an eternal state of readiness— like the constant and faithful lover it is ready to respond to our every call.

When I allow it, it is; when I avoid it, it is.

It requires no effort, demands no standards, and holds

As It Is

no preferences.

Being timeless it sees no path to tread; no debt to pay. Because it acknowledges no right or wrong, neither does it recognize judgment or guilt. Its love is absolutely unconditional. It simply watches with clarity, compassion, and delight as I move out for my return.

It is my birthright. It is my home. It is already that which I am.

As It Is

PRESENCE

If, however inadequately, enlightenment could be described in terms of qualities, I see them as unconditional love, compassion, stillness, and joy without cause. Existence in time is only a reflection of those qualities, and while I maintain and invest my belief in my separate identity, I can only again express a reflection of those qualities and not be their essence.

When I do not know who I am, I am bereft.

Enlightenment, however, has another quality, which is the bridge between the timeless and my illusory sense of separation. That quality is presence. Presence is our constant nature, but most of the time we are interrupting it by living in a state of expectation, motivation, or interpretation. We are hardly ever at home. In order to rediscover our freedom, we need to let go of these projections and allow the possibility of presence. Its real discovery, or our access to it, can only be made within the essence of "what is." This is where spontaneous aliveness resides, and where we can openly welcome the unknown.

Only here, in present awareness of simply "what is," can there be freedom from self-image.

To live passionately is to let go of everything for the wonder of timeless presence. When we are courageous

As It Is

enough to allow this, we suddenly rediscover that we are the sole source of all and everything.

Presence is not to be confused with "being here now," which is a continuous process of the separate self and has no direct relevance to liberation.

Presence is a quality of welcoming, open awareness, which is dedicated simply to "what is." There can still be someone who is aware and there is that of which they are conscious—the sound of running water, the taste of tea, the feeling of fear, or the weight and texture of sitting on a seat. And then there can be a letting go of the one who is aware, and all that remains is presence. All of this is totally without judgment, analysis, the wish to reach a conclusion, or to become anything. There is no mentation and no expectation. There is simply "what is."

At first, it is enough to allow dedicated awareness to "what is." Letting go of the one who is aware can easily follow, but it can never be a task.

I cannot "do" presence, simply because I "am" presence. So there is no process to learn because I cannot learn or achieve something that I already am.

Presence is totally effortless and is nearer to me than breathing. Presence can only be allowed and recognized. What I tend to do most of the time is sidestep it or interrupt it.

Existence would not be if it were not for presence. I am presence and you are presence. If we were not present, existence would not be. Presence emanates from the source of all and everything known or unknown. And that is what we are. We are the sole source of our own unique creation.

There can be presence or we can remain separate. There can be openness or we can invest in manipulation. There can be a welcoming of the continuous simplicity and wonder of simply "what is," or we can be imprisoned by the limitations of our expectations. All is appropriate.

Presence is the light in the darkness. It is atomic. One moment of presence brings more light to the world than a thousand years of "good works." In presence, all action is uncluttered and unsullied. It is spontaneity born from stillness.

In allowing presence, however, we embrace a kind of death. What dies is all expectation, judgment and effort to become. What dies is the stuff of separation, the sense of self-identity, which can only function in the illusory world of past and future, memory and expectation. For it will be found that if we let go into simply "what is," we will be in a place of unknowing.

That is how the embracing of presence is a kind of death. What dies is the dream of individuality. What we let go of is our incessant need to feel that we are a separate entity—that we will continue as a fraction of the whole. And, in that letting go, we come to see that all death is a rebirth into liberation.

For what we open up to in presence is the possibility of entering oneness, the rediscovery of what we really are. This is the bridge between the world of separation and enlightenment, which, once crossed, is no more.

When there is presence, the self is no more. We stand astride the living paradox and allow the emergence of freedom from the incessant movement toward becoming. It is a welcoming of the open secret.

When there is presence, there is awareness, and this is the light that dispels the apparent darkness. The light enters the darkness and dissipates those illusions that appear to interrupt oneness. Awareness does not divide or suppress and thereby gives energy to the unreal. It simply sees "what is" and brings the light which allows that which is illusory to evaporate.

Ↄ

There is never any situation in which we cannot be united with the present. Isn't that wonderful? I will say it again. Presence is available in any situation, or put another way, freedom is continuously available.

There is sufficient opportunity in every day to be present with pain, fear, the sound of a car, wind in the trees, my body in the chair, a pen in my fingers, emotional pain, habits, abounding self-judgment, guilt, walking, the taste of cheese, being in a hurry, being lazy, being in control, and the guru-mind which insists that presence is nonproductive and that I should be doing something "spiritual" or, at the very least, useful.

Presence shines wherever it will, on any part of existence.

If I try to bring light to one aspect of my story in particular, I disturb the natural flow and counterpoint of the opportunities that life and my innate wisdom presents to me. For presence is not a task—it cannot be used by my will. It is not a spiritual exercise or a tool to get somewhere, like prayer or formal meditation. When I attempt to harness it to a task, I have tried to constrain "that" which is beyond limitation.

CR

Presence is all-encompassing and is its own reward; it isn't trying to get anywhere. If I feel myself trying to get somewhere, then I have already interrupted it.

However, when there is presence, the whole being relaxes into its embrace. There are no more questions and there is no more striving. The mind departs its throne, the body relaxes, the breathing evens out, and the perception becomes global. I rest in that which never comes and never goes away.

When there is presence, there is total intimacy and the senses are heightened to a degree previously unrecognized; I see and touch in innocence, I taste and smell for the first time, and hear a new sound that is vital, fresh and unknown.

There is a subtle feeling of risk and serenity in

presence. It is the first and last step. It moves beyond time and self-identity and provides the ground in which the discovery of what I am is made immediately and directly available.

When there is presence, all that is illusory falls away, and what is left is real, vital, and passionately alive. This is life full on—not my life, not anyone else's life, but simply life.

Presence does not bring heaven down to earth or raise earth up to heaven. All is one.

As It Is

THE CHOICELESS
CHOICE

In presence, I see that I have never chosen or done anything, but that life lives through me.

And so I have never stopped the sea or moved the sun or taken one step nearer or further away from my birthright.

In accepting my divine helplessness, I enjoy the freedom of never having a past or future I could call my own.

Some people ask, "Who chooses, who directs this wonderful chaos?" But once in the arms of the beloved nothing matters, and I can live as though I choose and rejoice in the letting go.

My
World

In what I experience as my world, everything is totally unique for me. No one else can know my experience of the color red, my taste of tea, my feelings of fear and happiness, of walking, of dreaming, or of waking.

In time, my experiences largely shape my beliefs, and what I believe I again come to experience. It is the interplay of these two compatriots that seem to influence my life story, moment by moment, day by day, and so on.

At this level of existence, I appear to be the producer, scriptwriter, director of cast, script, and music in a film called "My Story."

When I look back at my life as openly as possible, I see how I have attracted to me the people, the events, and the patterns that have been perfectly appropriate to the kinds of influences and images that my particular belief systems have been expressing.

Many people have become very excited about this concept and have suggested and taught that if we can change our thought patterns and our belief systems, then we can change the way we experience life. It seems this could be so, but they also entirely miss the point, for who we really are is beyond the limitation of experience and belief.

Until I have rediscovered who I am, what kind of

As It Is

existence am I trying to create? From where do I see clearly that what I think I want is what I really need? Will my idea of what I should create be better than yours, or will our individual visions clash? That appears to be the recurring pattern.

What is possibly not realized by those who would pursue this concept is that beyond all of our wishes and desires to create what we think we want there is a hidden principle—the principle of unconditional love, which is continuously functioning, entirely inherent, but usually unrecognized. This principle is the very core of the living paradox.

All of existence as we know it, within the limitations of time, is only a reflection of that hidden principle which is continuously inviting us to remember what we really are. Within that reflection there is no right or wrong, better or worse, but only the invitation.

For while we remain locked within the experience of being separate individuals having to negotiate with existence, we remain in a state of dreaming.

In that dream state, all that we do is governed by the law of opposites, in which all that is seen as positive is exactly and equally balanced by its opposite. Through deep reflection, we come to discover that we are on a wheel in which everything repeats itself over and over again in differing images. What we apparently create we destroy, and what we apparently destroy we recreate again.

And despite what we might believe about free will

and choice, we come to see that we are dreamed characters in a divine play, reacting and responding from a set
of conditioned reflexes and belief systems. All of our
dream world that we see as progressive comes within the
parameters of this perfectly balanced and exactly
neutral state, which serves only to reflect the Divine
possibility.

We are the sole creators of this dream, which has
absolutely no purpose other than our awakening from it.

In reality, we are surrounded by and embraced in unconditional love, whether we respond to it or not. Our
experience in time sets up a perfectly appropriate
creation, exactly suited in its grand happenings and tiny
nuances to the particular and unique needs of our
reawakening. The source of the hidden principle is
ourselves, and it is fired by our longing to come home.

And however significant or insignificant we think our
activities are, however talented, artistic, useful, ordinary,
or fruitless we may feel our expression in the world
appears to be, all of this is simply and only a function of
that hidden principle: a totally appropriate reflection pro-
viding the never-ending opportunity to enter into it, see
beyond all phenomena, and rediscover the source of its
emanation.

THE DEATH
OF THE
BODY/MIND

The death of the body/mind is only the ending of the illusion of a journey in time.

The awakening to unconditional love is immediate. We are enveloped in our original nature regardless of anything that apparently happened.

When the body/mind is dropped, there is no intermediary process of preparation or purification. How can there be? Who was there? All ideas of a personal "afterlife" or reincarnation are merely the mind wishing to preserve the illusion of its continuity.

The story is over. The divine novel has been written and, regardless of how the mind might judge, not one iota could have been different. The scenery evaporates and the characters have left the stage—their apparent existence begins and ends with the dream that has been played out.

For we are the ocean and the waves, the darkness and the light.

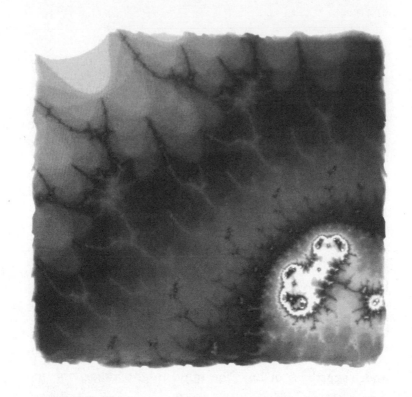

ABSTRACTION

I have been fascinated and waylaid by abstraction, dreaming about the life I would prefer to have, rather than living the experience of "what is."

What I abstract never really comes to be, it only sometimes flickers into life like a watered-down approximation. This abstraction is like a smoke screen born from longing or frustration, offering me a holiday of dreams. It is always safe, predictable, and an indulgence in the "known."

If I drop abstraction and move my awareness, for instance, to my bodily sensations, I discover there is a symphony going on. Not necessarily in tune, but nevertheless constantly changing and moving, coming and going. Something arises then disappears, followed by something else rising to take its place. There is very little that I can control or manipulate. It is immeasurable and unknown, coming into being then passing away.

In the same way, if I let go and listen, touch, taste, smell, or see, there is no way of knowing beforehand the exact quality of those sensations. I could say that I can anticipate the sound of a bird singing, but it is only information based on memory and is neither alive nor vital.

The sound I actually hear, the sound of "what is,"

As It Is

will not be the same as my abstraction of it. When I first listen to the sound I will try to grasp it and label it in order to control it. When I let go of that control, there is simply the listener and the sound. When the listener is dropped, there is only the sound. I am no longer there— there is simply the naked and vibrant energy of "what is." Nothing is needed; all is fulfilled.

It is within the very alchemy of this timeless presence that freedom resides.

Life beckons me. It whispers, calls me, and in the end it screams at me. The scream of crisis or disease is often what will bring me to the rediscovery of who I really am, for it is difficult to abstract suffering.

As It Is

FEAR

Until I recognize who I really am, my life can be largely driven by the things I fear.

It can be my fear that engenders my belief in a beginning and an end.

It is the fear of losing myself that can perpetuate and sustain my drive to survive and continue, and what I long for and fear most, is the absence of myself.

Fearing weakness I strive for control, fearing intimacy I strive to be aloof, fearing subservience I strive to be dominant, and if I fear being ordinary I try to be special.

The things I can be afraid of are endless, because if one fear is overcome I can put another one in its place.

If there is present awareness, fear is seen clearly as an abstraction—a future anxiety born from memory's blueprint. If the story that engenders the fear is dropped, I discover that all I am left with is a physical sensation that is raw and alive. Now it ceases to overrun me and quietly takes its place in existence. It is the same with physical or emotional pain. When I cease to own it I liberate myself from its bondage and see it simply as it is.

If I cease to label suffering as "bad" and "mine," and simply allow it as energy in a certain form, it can then begin to have its own flavor, which can take me deeply

As It Is

into presence.

The nature of suffering is that it speaks deeply to me of another possibility. By desiring pleasure and avoiding pain, I chop in two the very root of that possibility.

As It Is

GUILT

I can only feel guilty if I judge who I am from a set of belief systems that I have been taught or that I have constructed for myself. My self-constructed beliefs again can only emanate from my past experiences in time. These concepts are linked to the idea of a journey towards a goal, a path to purification.

In presence there is no becoming, no attachment to a goal. I see that I no longer have to achieve any standard or behave in a certain way in order to become worthy.

When I expend my energy in feeling guilty and attempting to assuage that illusory sense, I continuously negate the possibility of liberation. There is a fascination and an indulgence built into the drama of sin, or karma, which can powerfully mislead one from attempting the rediscovery of his or her true nature. What I am doing is investing in an illusory concept about right or wrong in order to avoid that which is absolutely beyond both.

In presence there is no debt because there is no history. In any situation, either I feel separate or there is presence. In separation, no matter what happens I feel separate. In presence, the self is no more and there is simply "that which is."

Either situation is complete. Each moment *is* its own reward. It is there and then it is gone. There is no further ongoing debt to pay.

When we continuously employ the remorseless judge to calculate and measure everything we do or are, we imprison ourselves in an existence of struggle, guilt, and suffering, trying to appease a god that is ourselves projected.

There is only knowing or unknowing. If I cannot "understand," I cannot see, and darkness is simply darkness, it is neither right nor wrong.

All concepts of good or bad, original sin, karma, or debt of any kind are the products of an unawakened mind that is locked into time and the maintenance and reinforcement of a sense of father, mother, and self.

As It Is

THINKING

My thinking creates time. Within time-thinking, I maintain my illusory sense of self-identity and separation. I think, therefore I continue.

Thought, which is time-based, divides the mind and continuously produces ideas of progress towards satisfaction or misfortune. It disturbs, yet speaks of order; makes promises, yet speaks of destruction.

My time-thinking moves backward and forward over a sea of memories and projections from a place that I call "myself."

My mind is seeking in every part of existence, in the seen and unseen, searching and longing, only to discover "the one that is looking."

No amount of thinking will tell me who I am, but understanding can take me to the river's edge.

Creative thinking emerges from stillness. Stillness is not brought about by the absence of thought; it is absolutely beyond the absence *or* presence of thought. I cannot make myself still, but when that which appears not to be still is seen, then that seeing emanates from stillness.

But if I move beyond thinking, where am I and who am I?

RELATIONSHIPS

My early experiences with parents and others set up my beliefs and my patterns about relationships, and these patterns follow and influence every relationship thereafter until I rediscover who I am.

In whatever game I play, those to whom I relate will, in the main, become compatriots in that game and reinforce and support it. If I need to be needed, I will create the needy. If I need to be rejected, then I will attract rejection. There are as many variations as there are people. But patterns are only a confirmation of my particular needs and beliefs, and they reflect that which I have not yet rediscovered. They are perfectly appropriate—simply a part of the hidden principle of unconditional love inviting me to see another possibility.

What I experience as a relationship in my world of time and separation seems like a link between another and myself. It can be an exchange of feelings, interests and enthusiasms, laughter and tears, thoughts and reflections. One part communicating with another part. I am relating to that which I project out there, apart from myself. There is very little merging in the fullest sense. It seems rather like a communication between two projections, two conditionings, two patterns, or an agreement to stroke each other's egos.

As It Is

When I first meet somebody, my computer sometimes places the other person in a box in which I keep him or her imprisoned. Sometimes I will extend bits of the box here and there, or I will make it bigger or smaller. In this way, I stay safe and relate to my concepts about the person rather than who they really are.

When I strive to become that which I think is my cause, I can live in a state of comparison with others or see them as my judge. It is a kind of subtle competition. I can also see the other person as someone who I believe can fulfill my sense of lack. They can acknowledge the image that I wish to project, or they can reinforce my sense of being worthy. They can excite me and comfort me with their presence. They fulfill a need.

The way in which I relate to others is a most powerful reflection in the most fundamental relationship of all, and that is with myself.

When I have rediscovered who I am, however, there is no longer any question of relationships. In this open and welcoming presence there is no need for memory or repetition, comparison or expectation—no place for one part meeting another. There is no distance between the two and therefore nothing needs to relate.

All of our energy is merged into a continual freshness, and the celebration of simply "what is."

It is a communion of spontaneous giving and receiving that can enlighten those times when we return to relating. Often there is silence because there is no need to fill the void once seen as threatening. These silences are full of simply being together in an existence that is continually dancing.

I AM NOT

I am not . . . my life story, the mind, the body, feelings, experiences of pain or pleasure, struggle, success, or failure. I am not loneliness, stillness, frustration, or compassion. I am not even what I think is my purpose, the seeking, the finding, or anything which is called a spiritual experience.

When I don't know what I am I sanctify these experiences, take ownership of them and give them great significance. I believe they mean something which, once understood, will provide me with answers and formulas. But these experiences are only consciousness concealing and revealing itself in order to be recognized. When I know "what" I am I discover that I am not existence; I am the presence which allows existence to be. Existence either blossoms in that presence or reflects back my sense of separation.

I Am

I am . . . the divine expression exactly as I am, right here, right now. You are the divine expression exactly as you are, right here, right now. It is the divine expression, exactly as it is, right here, right now. Nothing, absolutely nothing, needs to be added or taken away. Nothing is more valid or sacred than anything else. No conditions need to be fulfilled. The infinite is not somewhere else waiting for us to become worthy.

I do not have to experience "the dark night of the soul," or surrender, be purified, or go through any kind of change or process. How can the illusory separate self practice something in order to reveal that it is illusory?

I don't need to be serious, honest, dishonest, moral or immoral, aesthetic, or gross. There are no reference points. The life story that has apparently happened is uniquely and exactly appropriate for each awakening. All is just as it should be, right now. Not because it is a potential for something better, but simply because all that *is* is divine expression.

The invitation to discover that there is no one who needs liberating is constant. There is no need to wait for moments of transformation, to look for the non-doer, permanent bliss, an egoless state, or a still mind. I don't even have to wait for grace to descend, for I am, you are, it is already the abiding grace.

As It Is

Part II
DIALOGUES

Introduction to the Dialogues

"Words are not truth just as honey is not sweetness."

When we need to describe a simple way to cook an apple pie, mend a puncture, or to travel from here to there, verbal communication is entirely suitable. Describing any process, which has a beginning, middle, and an end, is straightforward—as meaning is conveyed on a raft of words, which diffuse into understanding in the mind of the reader. However, looking at language more closely, we can also see that it tends to reinforce a sense of separation, since in everyday use, language describes objects relative to places and processes.

When using verbal communication to describe awakening, enlightenment, nirvana, or whatever other word suits you, language can suddenly turn. At the same time the author is trying to convey oneness, the very words are pulling toward separation.

In speaking of liberation, with clarity, we are talking about something that is beyond the mind's capacity to understand. As liberation brings with it the realization that there has never been anyone to liberate, the mind perceives an increasing threat. Consequently, it will use

As It Is

its considerable guile to find a way to convince us that it first fully understands what is being suggested and, secondly, that it will gladly assist in delivering whatever fulfillment seems to be offered. This assistance will immediately be translated into a process. It needs to be stressed, again and again, that personal processes cannot open us to enlightenment. Nevertheless, the mind will even translate this statement into some sort of ritual, affirmation, or mantra.

During discussions, I suggest that people try to forget what has been said, because everyone has a particular intelligence, which already knows what is being expressed. I also suggest that you watch how the mind will keep on turning the pages, looking for that one answer that will do the trick.

It doesn't really work that way.

As more and more people hear this very direct message of the nature of awakening (despite all of the words), a deep inner resonance is taking place. Of course, clarity of perception has its place in all of this, but I see the darkness fall from people's eyes as a new and radical vision arises.

In the meantime, here are some more words . . .

Dialogues with Tony Parsons

You have written about "the open secret." Where does this expression come from?

When I walked across the park, one of the most amazing and liberating things that was seen was that everything was the ground of unconditional love. There is nothing that is not sacred, and, regardless of any particular state I might be in, I saw that grace was continuously available. Look, here is the secret (picks up a sweater and throws it on the floor). In the dream, we see a separate object. When there is no illusory, separate self, the ground of unconditional love is seen. This is what is always open and available to us. There is nothing that exists outside of the ground of this natural unity. The "secret" is that there is no separation, but it remains a secret as long as we believe we are someone.

How can I see that?

You can't see it until you stop looking for it, and simply let "what is" be there.

As It Is

How can I do that?

You can't "do" it. But you can open your heart to the suggestion that it can happen. Allow awareness simply to rest in "what is," whether it is a bum on a seat, or the frustration at not seeing, that's it. Simply allow "what is" and the ground of love will emerge to embrace you. It is always ready and willing, like the eternal lover, to welcome you into the infinite. There is no need to change or still the mind, or purify the body—simply, exactly as you are, is the divine expression.

But that sounds too simple.

We all know in our hearts that the answer to all of this is very simple. Christ said the kingdom of heaven is like a mustard seed. It is found in the very ordinary. That you are unique, here and now, is the secret. This moment has never happened before; do you see that? It is here and then it is gone and will never happen again. And now here is another moment. It is unique and it arises and then falls back into the infinite, never to be seen again. It is what you are; do you see that? You are the infinite expression, moving in and out. You cannot stop "what is"; it is a continuous and eternal dance—so let go and simply allow it.

Are you recommending that we bring our awareness to "what is" as much as possible?

I cannot recommend anything. I am suggesting to you

that you come to understand and feel the need to wonder at the nature of "what is" here right now. Come and see that this is the timeless nature of the infinite. See that the mind will try to turn what is being discussed here into another process. When I talk to people about simply being aware of "what is," the mind immediately locks into the idea of a process that should be practiced. The mind is always looking for formulas. There can be no process to become what already is, and so there is, of course, nowhere to go and nothing to do.

⚥

What have you got to say about formal meditation?
Who is it that is meditating? If you sit and close your eyes and search forever, you will never find a meditator. For what reason do you meditate?

To still the mind.
For what?

In order that I can be available for enlightenment.
So while you are there expecting, or even trying to be open for enlightenment, nothing will happen. The anticipation alone is enough to guarantee that. Anticipation is a function of the mind, which is attached to memory of the past and expectations about what will happen in the future. While this is occurring, there can be no possi-

bility of anything else arising. In one way, I can say to you that you can meditate or not meditate; it makes no difference.

But if I choose to sit and watch my breathing, surely this shows my devotion.

When you come to see and understand the nature of "what is," its simplicity, its immediacy, its uniqueness, and its transience, then it is also understood that there is no point in formal meditation. You're sitting at the kitchen table, drinking coffee and the thought comes, "I will go and meditate." Then you see that there is simply no point, because where you are is "what is." What *is* is, and so why go to find it upstairs? When this is embraced, it is possible that it will be recognized that what you are is absolute awareness—nothing more, nothing less.

I have a teacher who has a form of very simple and slow yogic movement, and I find it slows my mind and puts me into a space that feels very close to pure beingness.
So what?

So, does this have a value?
It has an apparent value in the wheel of life. But so apparently does jogging or eating vegetarian food. Let's be very clear about this. What is being communicated here, right now, is never going to be popular or draw lots of people. The mind needs a target, a place to go to, some

kind of hopeful journey. What I am suggesting to you is that you accept that you are helpless, and then something else can arise. There is nothing that you can do that draws you nearer to awakening. How can a supposed "doer" practice non-doing? I am saying that there is nowhere to go, because this is it.

CR

I find in my work as a therapist that, in general, people have a heavy history, all of which they are trying to drop in order that the belief systems they have adopted can be changed, and the future be better. This history is powerful when you are involved in it emotionally, and it is not easy to drop all of that and be here now.

It is impossible to choose to be overwhelmed or not—we are simply helpless characters in a novel, and if it is written that we are taken over by these emotions, then that is consciousness choosing to be taken over by these emotions. However, let's be clear about this. I am not talking here about "being here now." Being here now is a continuous process for everyone most of the time. If someone is imagining being on a holiday in the Caribbean when sitting at their desk at the office, then their imagination is creating the scene they want right now. If someone is trying to kick a ball into a goal, then they are being here now. If someone feels jealous of their girlfriend kissing someone else, they are being here now. What I am suggesting is that you become open to the nature and availability of "what is."

So can I ask you to close your eyes? Simply become aware of whatever is most upfront for you in your awareness—it may be the sound of my voice, or noises in the room, or feelings in your body or face. It can shift quite quickly through all kinds of phenomena and doesn't have to stay with one thing. Now let whatever is there be there, and drop the person that questions or judges or has expectations about it. Just drop altogether the person that is trying to work it all out or anticipate what is coming next. Let there just be a seeing of "what is." Keep it simple . . . just let it be there . . . (long pause).

Okay, now open your eyes. In that moment, where was your past?

Nowhere.
Where was your future?

Nowhere.
You see, what I am suggesting is that during that period we had together, there were moments when the self no longer existed—there was just "what is." This has no connection with "being here now." There is no "one" looking at "now" and there is no "here." Once the wonder of "what is" is recognized and embraced, then a dedication arises, and those moments of nonexistence will grow and grow in one's life. And while this is happening, the imagined sepa-

rate entity will begin to evaporate under the impersonal gaze of the watcher. The past and the future are simply part of the drama that keeps us locked into the illusion of being separate entities. Once the gate has opened into another possibility, then the real adventure begins.

But aren't you affected by the past, and don't you worry about the future?
There are characteristics within this body/mind, and there are memories of what seems to be a past, which can influence choices about what appears to be a future. But it is seen and accepted that not only is the body organism helpless about the so-called future, it is also seen and accepted that nothing matters anyway. All that *is* is this right now, and this is the infinite expression—there is no other. In six years' time, wherever the body organism is and whatever it is supposedly doing, there will still only be "what is."

Do you not, therefore, experience fear or anger?
Fear or anger can arise, but it is seen as part of the whole manifesting of consciousness. It is the game that is going on. There is a feeling, say, of anger, there is your face, rain is falling on the roof, she has just put her hand on her mouth, there is anger, and there is the sound of a car going by. It is all the infinite in play, and I am the light that allows that play to be—and so are you. When this seeing is happening, it is also seen that one doesn't "own"

anything. Therefore, the feeling of fear and anger is no longer associated with any one person; it is just the next thing happening.

So how is it for you?

When the self is no more, there is simply an abiding in the beloved. The game goes on and there is a response to the game. But the response comes from nowhere and goes to nowhere. And the game and the response *is* the divine expression. All and everything is seen and heard and felt as the beloved. And the beloved is the ground of all that is.

But who sees this?

No one sees it—it is simply seen. It is the "is-ness" of what we are. Whatever we do and whichever way we are, exactly as we are, is the beloved expression. It's a mystery to the mind, but once realized then all questions fall away, and it is seen that there was never anyone there.

But you are only expressing your belief.

I can only say to you that once "it" is seen it can only be lived and has no connection with doubt or belief. I am that, you are that, she is that, and the carpet is that.

Then why do we live in this desperate state of unhappiness if we are that?

Again, the answer only emerges when there is no longer

a question, but the nearest I can get to the answer in words is to suggest to you that we are unhappy because we do not accept that we are divided in two in order to become one again. It is a game consciousness is playing, and at times it doesn't seem very funny. Separation is the experience that consciousness chooses to have, with all of its diversity, and the game is to dance in and out of separation and unity.

Well, I find that makes me really angry.
So what is it that is angry?

Me, I am.
And who are you?

I am myself, Richard.
So are you your name?

No, but that is my identity.
But it is not constant and it arises from memory. It can change—and so who are you?

I am someone who thinks I should be enlightened.
Where is that someone?

Inside here (points to head).
So are you your thoughts?
(long pause.)

As It Is

It feels like that.
And are the thoughts constantly changing?

Yes, one minute I'm a saint, and the next minute I'm mundane.
And is this who you are?

Not really, because I seem to change a lot, and sometimes I'm in my body.
So where are you now?
(long pause.)

I don't know. I feel I can't find myself sometimes.
Is it possible there is no one to find?

I suppose so.
And is there something else that is looking at these thoughts?

Sometimes.
And who do you feel that might be?

Well, you say that the watcher is seeing what is happening.
But what do you feel?
(long pause.)

I don't yet know.

As It Is

And where is your anger?
It's not there anymore, and I feel a strange excitement about something I can't put a name to.

ଅଃ

So we are sitting here, comfortable and warm, talking about Enlightenment, but what about all the suffering that is happening?
Where is this suffering? I don't see it.

But it is happening in the world. At the moment, there are thousands of people being slaughtered or being thrown out of their homes.
But at this moment, this is only information that you are conscious of. How are *you*? What's it like there where you are?

That's not the point. When all those people suffer, why should I bother investigating my silly trips?
I am suggesting that you don't investigate them. Until you can see the nature of suffering, what can you do for anyone else? However, if you are determined to end suffering in the world, then you had better get started right away. You are wasting your time here. You have a huge task ahead of you that will never end. On the other hand, you could just start with your own suffering and see what happens.

As It Is

But don't you suffer?

There is suffering but there isn't anyone who owns that suffering. It doesn't belong to anyone; it is all happening in consciousness. What we are talking about here is the possibility of total poverty and total humility. One of the realizations that accompanies awakening is that there is no one there to be awakened.

As a consequence of this realization, it is seen that there is no one there who owns anything at all. This is total poverty. It's what Christ was talking about when he said that it is more difficult for a rich man to enter the kingdom of heaven than for a camel to move through the eye of a needle. Life is simply happening, and you are the absolute awareness of that life. There is no one there to hook into anything or to lay claim to anything. That includes suffering.

But how do I deal with my suffering?

It is not a question of "dealing" with it. It is the coming to see and accepting the idea of the self being illusory that eliminates the ownership of suffering. So let's see *where* that suffering is. Where is your suffering?

It's all around me when it's there. It takes over everything and turns it sour.

Can you tell me where it is now?

No, it's not here right now, but it hangs in the background, ready to jump out at me.

So there is that past memory which feeds the idea of a future threat. But where are you? And do you have a sense of it being there all the time?

Yes.

So tell me where you are right now.

I feel I am in my mind.

Where is your mind?

(long pause.)

In my head.

And where are you who sees that?

(long pause.)

I feel I am something that is looking at me answering this question.

And what is that place like; what is watching something answer this question?

It feels like a nothing that is just watching.

And does it have any other qualities?

Yes, I suppose it feels clear and blank.

And where is the suffering?

It is not there at this time—I just feel a sort of calmness.

As It Is

So is there a sense of that suffering just being something out there in the air?

Yes.
So is there no one who owns it?

It's just there, like my mind.
When we begin to allow the possibility of what we are to really emerge, we come to see that what we are is totally constant, still and calm. There is simply no agenda and there is no past and no future consideration—nowhere to go, nothing to do, and everything that we think exists to threaten or to please us falls away. What is happening here is atomic. When it (presence) is allowed, we not only lift ourselves out of a pattern of owned suffering, we also lift the whole of creation out of that illusory imprisonment. We see people suffering and wish to help alleviate what seems to be their pain. We can take practical action to try and help, and at a certain level this is absolutely appropriate. However, what we are also doing is reinforcing in them the sense that they own their suffering. This is also consciousness manifesting this particular happening.

When someone in this manifestation steps outside that particular perspective and sees another possibility, then there is an easing of all apparent suffering.

CR

Sometimes I am completely taken over by fear or suffering, and it seems that there is nothing I can do about that.
Then there is "what is," and there is nothing to do but be taken over. This is also the infinite expression. I have to also say that when there is the beginning of a new light, a different perception that is happening, this can quite often exacerbate a powerful playing out of our particular and deepest fears. The mind will often support the ego in order to maintain its existence. The mind will, for instance, fight against what is being shared here. For some people here, the mind will rebel against this approach in full force. These kinds of discussions are a direct threat to its assumed supremacy.

But why is liberation so difficult to obtain? Why is there this fight? Who is holding on to what?
You are holding on to your seeming existence. All your life you have been conditioned to survive, to maintain the species, to continue the apparent line. No one wants to die. Look at the great media message, which tells you to make your life work.

This is the great game: the infinite manifests through you as a dreamed character in a grand play called life, mesmerized into the belief that you are a separate individual, you therefore believe that you have to negotiate with existence. This is frightening, among other things. At an early age, you can feel threatened by existence. A sense of your mortality and vulnerability sets in,

As It Is

and from then on you are powerfully motivated to maintain the status quo, to keep it all going and make the best
job you can of it. You continue to choose the best way in
what seems to be a separate existence, and make it as
good as you can. When this doesn't seem to work, some
people begin to ask the question "who am I," and this is
when another big difficulty arises—because the answer
to this question seems to be in direct opposition to
everything they have believed and invested in. What you
are is nothing. What you are is beyond anything you ever
believed. You as a separate entity have no choice and no
free will. You are simply being lived through by the infinite in order to discover that you are the infinite. These
are such perplexing and threatening concepts that most
people reject them. When they are also told that there is
nothing they can do to rediscover their freedom, then the
whole thing becomes unacceptable to the mind.

*Surely karma comes into question concerning the amount
of suffering that anybody experiences.*
Is that your belief?

Yes, it is, and it is my experience.
One follows the other as surely as night follows day. If it
is for you to believe that your good or bad actions will
have a cause and effect, then that is how it will be for all
the time that you believe it. The experience feeds the belief
and the belief feeds experience. But be aware that belief

only functions effectively in direct proportion to the suppression of the doubt that it seeks to override. And both are transient. You may believe one thing for five minutes and doubt it for three, and then another belief will take place and this will dominate for a while. All the time that we live in a world of abstract thinking, we are blown around in a maelstrom of differing and often opposing worlds that are the making of our imagination.

When awakening happens, it is seen that karma pre-destination and so on are all part of the game that is played out through the illusory identification of the separate entity. It is the infinite expression experiencing itself in limitation.

But surely I can choose to act in what I, at the time, feel to be a good way rather than a bad way.
Well, you can attempt to, but you have no real choice, simply because there is no one there to choose. All that is there is a dreamed character in a novel who will respond or react to any given circumstance in the way that the author chooses. These actions will be, to some extent, characteristic, but will also be influenced by the conditioning and belief systems that ensue at the time.

Who is the author?
Consciousness is the author and that is what you are.

So does consciousness choose a good or bad action?

Consciousness simply is. It is energy manifesting without any interest in any of the concepts that our minds have about good or bad, purpose or meaning. It is absolutely impersonal and has no particular direction. It is playing the game of creation and destruction.

But what about the novel?
The novel in a way is illusory because it has no beginning, middle, or end, and it is really just energy happening timelessly. Consciousness chooses to have varying and different experiences for no other reason than simply to have them.

So we are not going anywhere?
Nothing is going anywhere, and nothing is happening in time. There is only "what is, as it is." But see for yourself "who" it is that's asking. These kinds of hairsplitting questions are simply another way for the mind to avoid "what is." Simply rest in not trying to know the answer to everything. Wanting to know the answer is a way of trying to be in control. We are only exchanging concepts here. There is some clarity that can arise, and there are some beliefs that can be discarded. But "who" is asking about what consciousness wants and where it is going? Is it that you want to know all the rules of the club before you join? Do you want to see if it is right and proper before you say yes? You can't do anything about it.

You are life and that is all you are. You are the

infinite expression, and even as you ask the question, it is possible that you can see the answer in the question. Drop asking "why" and simply become totally involved in the absolutely wonderful miracle of life just as it is, right here, right now. Can you not see that whatever has just happened for you at this moment has never happened before and will never happen again? It is totally unique and fresh and innocent, and it is here and then it isn't. Isn't that great? And there, it's happened again, and you have just missed it because you want to ask another question about consciousness and its purpose for little old you. Just drop the head game and let it all be. The question and answer syndrome can be endless, and the mind often persuades us that the next answer that's on the next page might do it for us.

You don't need this imaginary person any longer, you know. This person that goes on and on and on asking questions, judging everything, calculating everything— just drop it. You have never ever needed that person, except that it brings you to this moment sitting here, hearing that you have never needed that person. Now drop it forever and simply allow life to happen without there being any illusory central datum or fixed point. Give up control and live in chaos. Fall in love with this, right here, right now. Be totally in love with "what is" and drop the supposed story that seems to bind together this imaginary someone and makes him or her seem real. It seems all so important and meaningful, and yet it signifies

As It Is

absolutely nothing at all.

$$\text{C\hspace{-0.3em}R}$$

What would you say about choice?
When awakening happens, it is seen that there was never anyone there to achieve that awakening. It is also recognized that throughout the life apparently previously led, there was never a "chooser" or a "doer." Everything that happened, from the tiniest nuance to what seemed to be the most major decision, could not have been any other way.

So there's no right or wrong way to do anything?
There is no longer any question of right or wrong at all. It is seen that the apparent separate entity is only a dreamed character in a novel that is being lived through by the divine energy, which is all there is. That apparent separate entity has certain predispositions and characteristics, and the choices are brought about by the conditioning and history of that lived character.

So what about free will?
There is no question of there being free will, simply because there is no one there in the first place who can have a will or make a choice. Ask yourself where do thoughts come from, and if you watch for some time you will see that they are not yours. They emerge, seemingly

As It Is

from nowhere, and rise up, have their time, and then recede to nothing. Their origin is not of your making.

So I might as well sit here and do nothing.
But in a way that is another apparent choice. You cannot help breathing, and you won't be able to do anything about getting up and walking out of this room. Everything is simply happening through you. There is tremendous relief when this realization is embraced—all guilt falls away, there are no longer any regrets, and it is seen that you have been brought to sit here and hear this. All struggle can drop away, and the effort to make one's life work suddenly loses its attraction. To relax and let life flow opens one to another possibility.

But how do I pay the mortgage?
It need not be a problem. The way in which the body/mind functions simply continues. Nothing apparently changes, but everything is transformed. In spontaneous creativity, without fear can come a deep harmony with what is happening. But this always has to be a secondary consideration and is never guaranteed.

But how do I know what is right or wrong for me and my loved ones?
You will not know and neither have you ever known. Be open to the idea of living the rest of your life in chaos; give up not having to know anything anymore. It is

As It Is

wonderful. You can only follow what seems obvious for you. Your work, your relationships, etc., all have a certain characteristic about them, which is generated through you by consciousness. Your life story has happened exactly as it needed to—it has been totally appropriate. That will continue and nothing you do will be right or wrong, it will simply be "what is." So relax and let it all happen—because it will anyway. The relief is letting go of this apparent inner voice, which is telling you how you should act or be. Just drop it now, right here. It's a fallacy that simply gets in the way.

As far as loved ones are concerned, you can only live through what you understand. You have no responsibility in any way for anyone or anything. There is no one there, and there never has been anyone there who can take responsibility.

Are you saying that we have no responsibility for anything?
What do you think?

I think that I have been a participant in the creation of my daughter, and so I should help her to live in the world as best she can.
That's probably all you can do at this time, but how were you a participant in her creation?

I was her mother's lover, and it was my seed that joined with her egg to begin it all.

As It Is

Who chose to make love to the mother?

*I did, although it was probably mutual in those days
(laughter).*
Where did the thought come from to make love?

It was more like an urge.
What was it that instigated the urge within you?

*When I think about it now, it seemed and still seems to
emerge from nowhere in particular.*
And so let's suggest please that the conception was
totally beyond your will—it simply happened.

Maybe, possibly.
So where was, and is, the urge first noticed?

*A kind of vibration begins in my body, followed by the
thought "I would like to make love."*
Where does it originate?

I don't really know.
So who receives it and takes responsibility for it?

I do.
What part of you?

Well, my body and then my thought.

As It Is

So which of those is you?

An amalgamation of those things.
So are you a mixture of different urges and thought?

It feels like that.
So what are you aware of right now?

Excitement.
Are you excitement?
(long pause.)

No, it's okay, I've got it already.
Got what?

I see I am that, which watches the excitement happening.

CR

Don't you think it is a good idea to use formal meditation as a way of clearing the mental traffic in order that the body/mind is more receptive to the energy of enlightenment when it happens?
If formal meditation happens, then it happens. There is nothing you can do about it anyway. However, it is possible to understand that there is no one in there who can choose. It can also be seen that the idea of mental traffic and the body/mind is an illusion. Go deeply into

As It Is

your awareness and keep asking "who" is it that will meditate. Who is it that owns mental traffic or emotional blocks? Where do they come from? Where does any thought or emotion come from? Also, once there is a dedication to "what is," then this becomes a continuous and living meditation, and thereafter there seems to be no reason why one should formalize it. It is happening in this room right now. Everyone is meditating and every one is meditation. Come to see that as you ask a question, the very use of the voice is the infinite expression. The answer is not needed—but then again your listening to the answer is also the infinite expression, whether you understand the answer or not.

Are you saying that therapeutic processes of, say, counseling, rebirthing, etc., are of no value in preparing someone to be more open to liberation?
There is no one to prepare for liberation, as there is no one to be liberated.

Okay, but isn't someone who is happier with themselves more open and available?
All we have is someone who is happier with his or her self. There are no rules. No conditions are required prior to awakening. We are talking here about an energy, a light, which is the source of all that is. This energy is impersonal. It is totally disinterested in what is apparently going on for an illusory body/mind. In fact, what is going

on is nothing. It is only dreamed. I would say that the divine energy can sweep everything away in one timeless gesture, but that is not necessary. Darkness is only "apparent"—it is the illusion of there being no light. There aren't different textures or levels of darkness. When light appears there is no darkness. And just as there are no levels of darkness, so there are no levels of progress towards light.

The problem with therapy is that it presumes there is a problem. In psychological terms there seems to be a journey from dark, through gray, to a lighter gray, which is more bearable. Someone can appear to progress from an uncomfortable or even distressing state to a better one—this is how consciousness wants to experience itself. But as far as awakening is concerned, nothing is actually happening because awakening emerges when the apparent separate self is no more.

But what about such things as yoga? Surely these techniques can bring one nearer to an acceptance of nothingness.

A separate entity cannot draw itself nearer to its own destruction. The doer cannot carry out a practice in order to discover the non-doer. However, everyone's experience is uniquely and exactly appropriate for them, and if that includes meditation or yoga, then that's what will happen. Everything that is apparently happening contains the invitation, including eating a hamburger, flying a kite, or sitting in the lotus position. It is only our intention or expectation that gets in the way.

Are you suggesting that awakening can happen to anyone at any time, regardless of what state they are in?
Yes, I am. In fact, I know of someone who was an antique dealer and who had absolutely no interest in anything that we are talking about here. When driving her car during her business activities, awakening simply happened, and afterwards she could only describe the happening as an overpowering sense of simply moving into the background with everything else seeming to be in the foreground. In her case, it totally changed her life. This certainly doesn't always happen, and some people continue in the same way as before but simply have a totally different perception. Let's be clear about this: the infinite is all there is, and as a consequence the rules or standards that our minds would set up for any kind of awakening simply do not apply.

So there is no way that we can prepare ourselves in order to be better receptacles.
Again you are seeing this only from the point of separate individuality. There are no receptacles—you are already the infinite expression. All you can do is come to see that there is nothing for you to do. That is a huge step; it is revolutionary.

CR

I find that sometimes in formal meditation there seems to be no one there anymore, and there is simply a vast open nothingness, which also feels very alive. But when I cease this meditation and come back to my everyday life, that space is not apparent. How do I reconcile these two situations?

This presence is available in any situation, and when it is first known it seems to be very intense and powerful. When light dissipates what seems to be darkness, there is an initial impact, which is very recognizable. However, as light becomes more constant and there is less apparent darkness, there comes about an acceptance that this is the natural way to be. As the light overtakes the darkness, the need to formally meditate becomes less. Also, it is seen that there are periods of natural awakeness and periods of apparent sleep.

Once it is accepted that all is the infinite expression, then these different periods simply do not matter anymore. When there is still a need for there to be one and not the other, then full realization has not yet happened—and that is also the infinite expression.

You speak of light dissipating darkness as though it is a process in time. Is this a contradiction about there being no process?

"No process" refers to the realization after awakening;

that no one could have achieved it, and no process could make it happen. In another way, everything we do and are could be called a process that brings us to the river's edge. Everything is an invitation. And it is seen that there is no one who can do anything about bringing either of these happenings about. It also seems that light dissipates apparent darkness through a period of what we believe to be time. However, when it is happening, it is happening within the timelessness of "what is."

≂

Many masters recommend meditation as a way of stopping the mind or certainly moving beyond it. What do you think?
Why stop the mind?

Because it takes me away from the peace and serenity that I long for.
Where is the mind right now?

It is right here speaking to me, questioning and analyzing what you are saying.
Do you feel that is the mind's job?

Yes. Primarily, it's what I use to understand and control what's going on in my life.
And where are *you*?

As It Is

I am here (points to head) in the information that is allowing me to answer this question.
So do you live in your head with that information all of the time?

Most of the time I spend most of my day in thought.
And who is it that sees that it is like that?

I do.
And so you see the mind working and thoughts arising and receding.

Yes.
And is that activity who you are?
(long pause.)

No, it doesn't feel exactly like that.
So do you get a sense of something that watches these activities arising and receding?

Sort of. It feels as though there is something above and behind that is watching right now.
Okay, so what is that place like?
(long pause.)

It's like a blank that is totally without concern for what's happening.
No judgments.

No. Simply seeing.
What do you think that is?

It feels to me that it's the bottom of all that I am.
And what does that feel like?

Very still but also very alive.
So that's your home, that's it, it's already what you are.
(long pause.)

Yes, that's it! And I have known it before but it seems to come and go.
Really, what we are has nothing to do with still minds, death of egos, purification, or any of the ideas we have been taught about states we should be in. This kind of teaching has to do with personal predispositions. It's always attractive to the mind when it is offered a method or a technique like stilling the mind or killing the ego. There is no possibility for the mind to still the mind, and once it is recognized that what you are is the still, silent awareness that sees the mind and its activities going on, then it is also recognized that there is no need to still the mind. It's all very simple, really—what we are is just the background, just sitting there waiting for us to stop somewhere and see the busyness. Once that happens, then we begin to have a different taste about what we are.

There have been enlightened masters who have had great charisma and who have also been capable of magic, manifestation, and so on. People have reported very powerful physical, emotional, and mental experiences not only in the master's presence, but even thousands of miles away. What is that all about?

It's about someone who has a lot of charisma and the gift of manifestation or magic. It's about nothing more than anything else of any relevance inside the wheel of life. Someone recently told me that she looked into the eyes of a so-called master and vanished for a moment. But if it meant anything, why was she still asking questions? Nothing of any relevance is happening here with these phenomena that is any different or more liberating than selling hamburgers in the marketplace. The difficulty arises when people believe that these kinds of events somehow vindicate some sort of personal enlightenment. Subsequently, they come to revere these people, and this creates a schism. They see these apparently magnificent beings and immediately come to believe that they can never attain such a level of importance. This is another way in which awakening is avoided. It is, of course, the infinite expression again wishing to have this experience, but so is my response to this question, and so is your sitting there and hearing it.

What does that mean to me?
Ask yourself what is being said here, and how it can bring clarity.

In what way?
Okay, here is a rug on the floor — there's nothing special about it—it's just a rug, very ordinary. I am suggesting to you that it is the infinite expression; it is the gateway to liberation. It is possible for you to open your eyes and to see in this rug that there is no separate self. That is what the rug is telling you—isn't that amazing? Just a rug, which can tell you and give you more than all the riches this world can offer. You will see something that will totally transform your whole perception of life. Something that is greater and more wonderful than anything you can imagine. On the other hand, given the gift, I could turn this rug into solid gold and give you something probably worth thousands of dollars. Which of these gifts do you want?

I can't give you a golden rug, and I wouldn't want to insult this magnificent thing lying on the floor that can tell us so much.

What we are talking about here today is the ordinary— the incredibly breathtaking magnificence of the ordinary. It is only ever and always simple, seemingly unremarkable, and right here and now. Immediately, here is the seeing of what we are. If there is a need in people to see magic, there will always be magicians to fulfill that need, but none of this is relevant to awakening.

But don't these people use something like an invitation card that can attract people to them, in order that later on they can help them towards enlightenment?

No one can help another toward enlightenment. It is not an issue like Bill teaching Joe to drive a car. In a shared openness it is possible that the illusory belief systems that can confuse people could fall away in a new understanding. But there is no one there trying to help another; comprehension is simply happening in that immeasurable spaciousness. However, if someone believes that they have become personally enlightened, which is a contradiction in terms, and they feel the need to help other people, then that will probably happen. The communication will be dualistic in its nature, and it will attract people who still have a need to be confused. I know someone who was with an Indian guru for many years and who had enjoyed many "spiritual experiences." This reinforced his sense of what he thought were significant happenings. He now finds it very difficult to live without that reassurance, and he certainly finds it very difficult to relate to the ordinary.

So what do we look for in a teacher?

Someone who gives you absolutely nothing and leaves you feeling helpless. Then it is possible that you are left only with "what is." If someone tells you that there is something that you can do or there is a certain way that you can be in order for awakening to happen, they are simply feeding your own avoidance.

What do you mean by that?
We all have a deep longing and a deep fear of the discovery of what we are, and the mind devises any way it can to avoid this discovery. The most effective way it avoids awakening is to seek it.

But surely there has to be some kind of drive in order to find this thing.
Again, there comes an acceptance that you can do nothing about this situation. If there is drive, there is drive. If there is not, there is not. But the emergence of liberation is not affected by either state, and once you come to believe you have to be a certain way; you have entirely missed the point, and so has your teacher. Of course, this is all the game of consciousness and doesn't restrict the possibility of awakening. But, you are sitting there listening to, and possibly hearing, that there is nothing you can do, and certainly understanding this can bring you to the river's edge.

So, in a nutshell, there is nothing that I can do?
You just need to see that you cannot *do* anything to be what you already are; just open your eyes and see that *this* is it. Even your question is the answer to your

question. Your voice, as you speak—the sound of it; the feel of it; the waves of sound and your particular, unique timbre, its vibration across the room and other people hearing it—that's it! Forget the question; all suffering emanates from the question "Why?" Just let the question be there because it is the answer. What has just happened is unique and transient, and simple and wonderful. And the hearing of it by us is also the answer to all our longings. It is here, it is this, it is now; it is already what you are.

CR

What is the difference between consciousness and presence?
There is absolutely no difference between consciousness and anything else in or out of existence. They are all one. However, for the sake of communication, I use the word *presence* to express as nearly as I can that sense of something that is absolutely still and silent, which is impersonal and ever constant, and from which all and everything emerges. It is what you are.

You talk about presence being a quality of enlightenment. Can you talk more about that?
The way I speak about the qualities of enlightenment is inadequate, because the nature of enlightenment is impossible to describe. What I am attempting to do is to

describe to the reader a set of qualities which can at least be comprehended. In that comprehension, there may arise an insight which moves beyond words and the mind, and which opens the real eyes of the reader. I have tried to indicate that presence is a welcoming, open stillness, which is the ground of what we are. It is our nature. Through dedication to the awareness of "what is," there can come a moment when there is no longer a self or a seeker; there is simply "what is." Though constantly available, it becomes apparent in those moments—this is what I call "presence."

To whom does it become apparent?
To no one. It is simply there; it is seen. It appears to fill everything when the self is no more. There is no one who is aware of it; it is simply "as it is." And now we have again crossed over to a place, which is not comprehensible or expressible in words.

Do you believe that this is so?
No, I *am* that, just as you are.

What does that mean?
It means that once awakening happens, there is no longer anything to believe in or doubt. It is the ending of all questioning. From then on, everything is simply "as it is." There is no longer a wondering why, having to judge or wishing to change anything. Presence becomes

apparent in that situation.

So the self never returns?
Never in the same way. The perspective is totally different. There is a sense of someone called Tony Parsons,
who has certain characteristics and predispositions, but
there is no longer a sense of separate entity or a sense of
a datum from where Tony Parsons lives. Tony Parsons is
no longer the center of the universe or the imaginary
person who has to negotiate with existence. Tony
Parsons is simply energy happening in the game of
consciousness, like the sound of cars driving by, you
moving your head, and the sound of someone coughing.
It is as though "I am" is the context of all that is, and
Tony Parsons is part of the content. In that freedom,
presence resides and actually has no quality that is
describable.

☙

*Where does thought come into all of this? What is its pur-
pose?*
Thought originates in the infinite and returns to the
infinite. It is part of the game of creation. There are two
kinds of thoughts: abstract thought and natural or
creative thought. Abstract thought is concerned with the
apparent future and the apparent past—will I win the
lottery or die of cancer or should I meditate more regu-

larly. Natural thought is, for instance, "I need to place this piece of wood in that position in order to saw it in half," or, "I will fry these onions before adding rice." All of our thoughts are fed to us from consciousness. That is why we have no responsibility. If you watch in a day where your thoughts come from or how they happen, you will discover when you get to the root of them that they are not yours and that they did not originate from you. When we discover this, we begin to see that we have no choice and no free will. We are being lived through, and one of the ways we are lived through is with thinking.

The dream of separation is maintained through abstract thought. We are all born with particular characteristics, and our lives will take a particular form or shape. After awakening, nothing will basically change, and the awakened one will still follow a particular way of being. Abstract thought can still happen, but most of the time the watcher is there, and as these abstract thoughts arise, they are simply not hooked into. There is, most of the time, no identification with them. Natural thinking begins to take over, and what I call creative thought also emerges and is expressed in one way or another. Often this awakening can be expressed in direct teaching with others, but creative thought can be expressed in any field you wish to mention.

So how do we deal with abstract thought?
Again, you cannot "deal" with it. But as you open more

As It Is

to the awareness and acceptance of "what is, as it is," there will emerge a freedom from the restriction of being identified with abstract thought. This will happen without your intention, so you can give up any judgment about thinking and allow it to be there, without the idea that you can do something about it. Come to see that you don't have to do anything about thought. Ultimately, you will realize that you are not your thoughts, your mind, your body, or any other object, but that behind all of these is a still, constant, seeming nothingness from which everything emanates; this is what you are.

℞

Once awakening happens, is it then possible to be all-knowing?
This is a fallacy that is generated from either ignorance or the wish to manipulate people. Once awakening happens, there is no question of the need to know anything anymore. Knowledge is for the mind to assimilate and use in order to control; awakening brings with it the seeing by no one that all is unity. There is no one there anymore who needs to know anything. There is the celebration of the ground of being in all that is. Let's be clear here: "all there is" means all there is within the circle of awareness of the energy of what I am.

What does that mean?

It means that the creation is happening through the form of this seeing, this awareness that you might, for the sake of clarity, call Tony Parsons. I am the light that allows that creation to be—it is, of course, the whole world, the whole of creation within that awareness. You are the light, which creates your whole world. In other words, we are all gods, but most of us believe that we are individuals or part of the whole.

So you don't possess all-knowing or all-seeing power?
Why should I wish to? Once awakening happens, there is simply and absolutely nothing one needs to possess anymore—it is the end of all need. It is total fulfillment, but it is an ever-changing and alive fulfillment, not a fixed, perfect bliss as some would have us believe. There is something very dead about this concept. There is no longer any need to know anything, because there is no longer any need to get anywhere.

But if you want to help others, aren't these powers useful?
There is no longer any need or wish to help anyone. Everything and everyone is the light, the infinite expression, just as they are. I am trying to say to you that you don't need help. Just as you are is how it needs to be.

But we don't know that?
You don't know that? That is your reality, and "not knowing" is also an expression of the infinite.

As It Is

But don't you want to help me in my suffering?
I can't help you. I can't take you anywhere, because there is nowhere you need to go. I can only suggest that you begin to open to the idea that there is no one suffering.

So what are you doing here?
Nothing. There is no one here doing anything. There is energy in a form discussing something with energy in another form. That's all there is.

But if there is nowhere to go, there is no purpose, it seems, in anything.
And this realization is the beginning of liberation. We are so locked into the belief that our lives have some sort of purpose we have to fulfill. We go on struggling to fulfill ideas we have of something we need to do, or somewhere that we need to reach in order to be worthy for enlightenment. Of course we never get there, because we are trying to satisfy some idea that is only imaginary anyway. It's the seeking for something on a horizon that is continually distant. All of this activity reinforces the sense of individual striving, and so the game goes on. Any sense of there being no point to any of this activity is a threat to the mind, but when there is an acceptance and a resting in there being no purpose, a new wonder can arise.

ɔ

Am I a creation of consciousness?
Consciousness is all there is, and there is nothing that doesn't emerge from consciousness. The belief in a small self is consciousness identifying as a separate entity as "me." This is a game of hide-and-seek.

So I am illusory?
The sense of a separate entity is illusory. Presence is what you are.

So I can't be responsible for anything because I don't make choices?
That's how it is. How can an illusory, separate self, who has no choice, be responsible?

Why is there a sense of separation?
That is the game. The infinite is at rest, and then the infinite is at play. Part of that game, which you originated, is having the experience of feeling separate and then going home. This happens for everyone, but for most it happens at the point of the death of the body/mind. The infinite enjoys the experience of limitation, with the possibility of liberation.

Why?
There is no answer to this until there is no question. From the point of view of the separate individual everything seems unfair, but from the awakened point of view,

everything is appropriate.

But for those who don't awaken, there is always something missing.

There is not necessarily an awareness of anything missing. Many people haven't even heard of the word enlightenment, and although every desire in the end is the desire to return home, these people are being "lived through" by the infinite in their own unique way.

But they also suffer.

They suffer and they enjoy in direct proportion to their need. There is a unique balance for everyone, and so the swing between negative and positive creates this exact balance and invites people to look beyond what is happening to another possibility. At the death of the body, everyone simply returns to what they already are, which is the divine at rest.

Even people like Hitler?

Oh, absolutely. He, like everyone else, played out the character that consciousness chose, and death is simply a return to the source from where the character appeared. The beloved plays every part in the play; even the part that believes it is separate. At the end of the play the beloved is just the beloved. From the point of view of the separate self, everything is judged from a right or wrong attitude, and there seems to be a battle ensuing between good and evil. However, these apparent events and this apparent struggle is really only a metaphor for something that is beyond the apparent battle. Once awakening happens, it is seen that there is no such thing as right or wrong.

But all that you are saying is only conceptual.
Everything that is being discussed here is conceptual. The only thing that we can know is real is our presence. You see, you exist don't you? The beloved plays every part in the play; even the part that believes it is separate. At the end of the play the beloved is just the beloved. From the point of view of the separate self, everything is judged from a right or wrong attitude, and there seems to be a battle ensuing between good and evil. However, these apparent events and this apparent struggle is really only a metaphor for something that is beyond the apparent battle. Once awakening happens, it is seen that there is no such thing as right or wrong.

Yes.
Okay. So it appears that that is all that is going on here. However, there is also an intermingling and exchange of energy, and in these situations there can be an expansion and an openness that happens.

In fact, this openness is available continuously in any situation, but when two or three are gathered together to share in this kind of communication, then more than

As It Is

just concepts are being shared.

CR

You say that everything is the infinite expression, so that includes the carpets, the window, and your face?
Yes.

Are you at one with all those things?
Not at one in the way that one would imagine, but it is better to say "not in two."

So what does that mean?
When awakening happens it is seen (by no one) that all is unity. All and everything emanates from silence and unconditional love. So there is a transformation in perception. Suddenly there is no separate one there—only unity. Once that has been seen, then thereafter a ground of beingness, or unconditional love, is recognized in all that is. It is as though instantly, everything has about it a presence of love or a universal benevolence.

And is this a constant for you?
You see, time, longevity, doesn't really enter into this perception. For the sake of clarity, for me there is largely this perception but there is also contraction. This is the dance that is played. But there is a clarity here: that liberation and contraction are both absolutely okay. There

As It Is

is also, of course, a constant seeing that everything is the beloved. So there is never a feeling that one is lost. There are no more questions; there is nowhere to go, and nothing more to become. This is home.

CR

Does the ego get in the way of awakening?
Everything and nothing gets in the way of awakening. However, a great deal of confusion has been generated, especially from Eastern teachings, concerning the need to overcome the ego, the mind, thoughts, etc., and none of it is relevant. The ego, the mind, and abstract thinking, for instance, are all the infinite expression, and if any of these things are active, then they will be active regardless of the idea that you can have any influence on their manifestation. When awakening happens, then everything is seen as absolutely fine just the way it is. The mind, which is only really a collection of thoughts, simply goes on in its own sweet and often silly way, but there is no longer any identification with it. The ego tends to diminish in effect as the gaze of presence evaporates its illusory identity. Usually the ego demands full attention, like a child, and when it is simply gazed upon without any interest, it tends to dry up and die.

Isn't that gazing at the ego a kind of dualism?
When watching becomes apparent to the separate

entity, it seems at first to create a distance, and this gives one the sense of dualism. But there is no question of separation as far as watching is concerned. Be clear that we are not talking here about self-observation, but we are talking about the quality of watching, which is not of the self.

What is the difference between dualism and duality?
Awakening is the ending of the effect of dualism, which is the illusory experience of separation. Duality is the recognition that there is a wall over there, which appears to be an object but is also a reflection of the ground of all being.

So what is watching?
Watching is the constant gaze of consciousness seeing and delighting in its creation. Its nature is totally impersonal, and for the separate entity is only a gateway between the separation and being. When there is no longer a self and there is only being or presence, then watching is no longer there—it is simply a gateway. However, it is also not a process that can be taken up and used by the mind.

So I can't "do" watching?
You can't do anything because you can't "do" what you already are. You are the light, which allows creation to be. Look, it is happening right here, right now in everything that's taking place for you. Simply let it be there. *Allow* the watching to happen and let it see what is happening.

As It Is

No questions, no judgments, no wish to change anything or make it better.

Fall in love with this. Fall in love with it intimately, and everything else will emerge. And don't stay fixed with one thing. Let whatever arises come to the forefront and fall away back into emptiness.

ॐ

Is a guru needed at all?
Life is the only guru. Everything that has happened to you so far is your teaching and is absolutely appropriate for your awakening. At this moment, it is sitting in this room and hearing these words and possibly allowing them to go deeply inside. It is the seed that is scattered and drops onto fertile or infertile ground. You are ready to hear when you are ready to hear. You don't need anything except that which you have. Isn't that wonderful? So don't get worried about what you need or don't need. All is provided. Let go and rest in "that which is," and you will surely meet the beloved and rediscover your original nature.

Then there isn't anything that would harm my awakening?
Everything leads to awakening. Even what your mind may see as harmful is reminding you of another possibility. Simply give up your attachment and fascination with

the story and let life happen. Something else of immense significance will take the place of all your worries, and you will be overrun by a new sense of wonder. Everything will reflect a quality of benevolence. This is the natural way for life to be.

Have you noticed a particular quality in people who have awakened through your work that you can tell us about?
Who is asking? If I said this or that quality could bring awakening, would the mind then try to invoke that quality? People who have awakened have not done so because of my work; they have simply awakened. However, I would say that there is a kind of childlike innocence and a readiness to wonder. But we all have these qualities; they don't have to be manifested or worked upon. It is simply that sometimes they have been mislaid.

How can you recognize a real or true guru?
You can't. You can, however, come to see that there is no such thing as the truth, there is only "what is, as it is" right now. Whoever you meet along the way, that's how it's meant to be. If you sit with someone who appears to be a great master but speaks from ignorance, that is the infinite expression. If you listen to someone who is awakened and speaks with clarity, that is also the infinite expression, but there is no guarantee that you will hear. For some people, they feel the need to be with somebody

who seems to be very special and magical and important. I would say seek out a teacher who gives you nothing at all, no hope, no method, no personal offer to take you there, because of course there isn't anywhere to go.

Look for someone who destroys all of your belief systems and who is always throwing you back onto "what is," right here. Any teaching that advises you that you need to be serious or honest or purified or changed through some process is simply not relevant. I have met people who have been with very powerful Eastern teachers and who have had many so-called spiritual experiences. These people have considerable difficulty in accepting and living with the idea of the divine being in the ordinary. They still seek the excitement of these so-called spiritual experiences and have very little time for the idea that a single footstep could be miraculous. As a consequence, they are often a bit lost in the ordinary world and still look for the extraordinary wherever they can.

But isn't enlightenment an extraordinary thing?
No, not at all. That is the point. Enlightenment is our natural and ordinary way of being. In comparison with separation, awakening is extraordinary. Suddenly there is no longer a feeling of alienation. Nothing in particular changes in one's life except the perception of everything. Give up the idea of bright lights and fireworks, and that awakening is something extraordinary and almost unavailable. Simply lie back and rest in the lap of "what

is." And then it is possible that your eyes will open and a huge gratitude will fill you.

CR

What can I learn from you that I can't learn on my own?
Nothing at all. You understand everything that is being discussed here, but you may not necessarily acknowledge it. What you *are* requires no learning. The "apparent" separate entity, however, is being told that it is an illusion. The belief systems are perhaps being demolished, and the idea of hope, success, or failure is being vanquished, together with the concept of good and evil. All that is left is nothing. "Nothing" does not have a need to learn anything.

You are the divine manifestation, so where is learning needed? You don't need me or anyone or anything. If someone suggests to you that they can take you to awakening, then simply walk away. Where do they have to take you when you are already that illumination?

So how do we begin to allow what we are to emerge?
It has already begun. Your very question, your very longing, is the seed. The seed contains all potential for awakening, and once it is in the ground, it can be fed by your expansion into absolute awareness. Each time you let go of the abstract mind and be with "what is," you water the ground and the seed continues to grow. Every

time you see the illusory nature of your conditioning, you create the space into which fulfillment can grow. During this time you are on the bridge, and your old fears may rise up and try to fight. But as you come to see the wonder and timelessness of "what is," these old struggles begin to lose their grip and something new takes their place.

What is enlightenment?
There are no words that can describe enlightenment. It brings with it, however, the realization that there was never anybody or anything to be enlightened.

And yet some people are enlightened and others are not.
There is no "person" that is enlightened; that is a contradiction in terms. There is no separate self and there is already light. You are the light, but you believe in the illusion of yourself as separate. Simply drop seeking and there it is. There is absolutely nothing to look for.

What is the seeker/teacher relationship?
Again, there isn't one. In awakening, there is no relationship, because relationship implies two apart who have some kind of agreement to be with each other. If the so-called teacher is no longer invested in separation and has moved beyond the illusion of self-hood, then who can relate? What is seen in that form by the seeker is freedom, spaciousness, and a celebration which resonates.

As It Is

This is only recognition of what the seeker already is. You are the light; simply rest in that and celebrate your natural birthright.

So what do you see that I do not?
Nothing different, but what is seen is uncluttered. It is simply "what is." However, in what is seen is also the "is-ness" of unconditional love, the ground of being. It is seen in all and everything, be it a so-called beautiful sunset or a trashcan. Everything exists in light and emanates from the silence of source. There is absolutely nothing that doesn't generate this ground of being. All is sacred, and we walk and talk and have our time in that which is no less than heaven.

But do you know anymore than I do?
This is not a question of knowledge at all. It is the seeing of something that never comes and never goes away.

Can this wonder be approached?
It is already "this." In what way can it be approached? As the illusory individual apparently moves towards something that is thought to be over there, the point is lost. What is sought is in the very movement of the seeker. As the reader reads these words, it is "as it is."

That is so beautiful; why can't I accept it and let it be like that?

As It Is

You are already "that which is." But your mind is frightened to let go and still has an idea that something special should happen.

So what can I do?
Begin to allow the watcher to emerge. See that the mind is always trying to run the show, to strut the stage. Just see this without judgment, and that seeing emanates from silence. This is what you are. It's like a film projector that is always on. We put the film through the projector and it plays out the life story with all its ups and downs, its dramas and conflicts, which we are fascinated by, but which signify nothing. Then the film runs out; the light is still on. You are the light.

I would invite people here to simply close their eyes and allow awareness to rest wherever it will. It will be discovered that awareness rests in one place only and then moves to another place and so on. Don't try to fix awareness anywhere in particular, because again this is the mind trying to indulge in a process.

Awareness can alight on sounds, in the body, on emotions, back to the sound of a car, and then on to the breath, and so on. Thoughts can arise and recede, and awareness will again alight wherever it will. Now notice that if there is a real intimacy with awareness of "what is," then it is seen that it only rests on one point, and everything else is diffused. This one point is what I call the life point. This is "what is, as it is." It is the invitation, the gateway. There can still be an apparent someone who is aware, but it is very possible at this juncture that the apparent someone will vanish, and there will only be "what is." Here is absolute awareness. The invitation has apparently been accepted. The door, it seems, has been knocked on and has apparently opened. In reality there is no one knocking, and there is no door that has to open.

So can I choose to be aware of "what is" in order to accept the invitation?
You can apparently choose to be aware, but it will eventually be recognized that there was never a "chooser" or a doer.

By "whom" will it be recognized?
By no one. It will be seen by absolute awareness, which is what you are.

So is this being in the now, or living in the moment?
No, it is absolutely not being in the now or living in the moment. This terminology implies that there is someone who can be, or live in, something called "now" or "this moment." Both ideas are illusory. There is no separate someone who can intentionally do anything, and there is no such thing as this moment or now. Where is *now*? Where is the next *now*? Now implies that there could be a then, so where is then? Now and then are both time

concepts. When there is only "what is," without apparent separation, then there is absolute being, or presence; and this timelessness, this light, this silence and utter stillness is what you are. Many people have come to hear these words, and as they open to this possibility, moments of presence take them over.

જી

How did your teacher help you?
I have never had a teacher or seen anyone as a master. I knew when I was a kid that life must be the teacher. I prefer the word invitation. This was confirmed when walking across the park.

Surely you needed to understand something from other people's writings.
Oh, yes. My first really deep understanding, which came from reading, was an interpretation of Christ's words in the book *The New Man*, by Maurice Nicholl. He explained that the word "repent" did not mean, "to show sorrow for your sins and vow never to sin again." The word, in Christ's native local tongue, meant "to turn 180 degrees and see anew." This was for me a revelation that went deeper than just intellectual understanding. At an early age, I knew that there was a secret, and I sensed that Christ knew and lived this secret, and that much of what he said referred to it. After walking across the park, other

people's writings on this subject were there like a confirmation for me, and I also learned from these people how to communicate in a clearer way.

What else did you learn through your readings about Christ?
At this time, I also came to understand the meaning behind the symbolism of the Christian cross. Life is *apparently* a horizontal journey through something we call time. It seems to swing between negative and positive experiences, and while we believe we are separate individuals, we try to make our lives as positive as possible. However, as I see now, everyone has exactly the experiences of either polarity that they need, regardless of their efforts to influence that balance. The apparent horizontal journey has only one purpose, and that is to invite us to see another possibility. That other possibility is the realization of verticality. We are the vertical line that intersects the horizontal line. We are the light that lives within the ordinary living experience. And this is what the crucifix signifies.

Anything else?
Yes, the forgiveness of sins. I feel Christ spoke directly to his disciples about these things, but what he said to the people was often hidden in parables. When he told people their sins were forgiven, he was really saying to them that they had never had a past that they could be held

As It Is

responsible for. They had simply been characters lived through by the infinite, never having had any choice or free will.

Do you feel that any attempt to organize any of these concepts immediately devalues them?
The secret that's available, and which you are anyway, can never be devalued. The written word cannot reveal the secret because a secret is a living, vital, timeless treasure. But the mind will protect itself by appearing to support the communication being made. The avoidance of what is most feared is created by turning what is being communicated into a method or system, which can be formulated, packaged, and delivered to groups of people. This has happened through history and is happening today with teachers who wish to control groups of people.

For instance, some teachers give people new names, and of course this still reinforces the sense of individuality linked with a new, but still separate, identity. Groups are formed, and either people live together in ashrams or belong loosely to an organization. As a result of this, there is created a feeling of specialness and exclusion from the rest of the world. This appeals very much to the guru-mind. It is also a very effective way for the secret to remain hidden until it can emerge, when appropriate.

It feels to me that you have something that I don't, and I want to get there as quickly as possible.

As It Is

Firstly, you can't get quickly to where you already are (laughter). But really take this in. Live with it and try to see deeply what it is really saying. The problem is that you think something has to happen. You are waiting for something to happen. It is actually happening continuously, and you simply don't see it. I don't have anything that you don't have. The difference is that I am no longer looking for anything. This is it, and that's the end of it. Give up the search for something to happen and fall in love, fall intimately in love with the gift of presence in "what is."

Here, right here, is the seat of all that you will ever long for. It is simple and ordinary and magnificent. You see, you are already home.

ABOUT THE AUTHOR

TONY PARSONS was born in London in 1933. At the age of twenty, he spontaneously awoke to the rediscovery of his true nature. Throughout the years he shared this "open secret" with like-minded friends. Only since 1996, when Tony began to communicate the nature of his experience through writings, did people from all over Europe begin to deeply resonate with the message he shares.

Tony brings a deep maturity and lifetime of spiritual understanding to his talks and published works. The clarity and completely natural manner in which Tony Parsons writes and speaks—about living in the unlimited Awareness of the present—is refreshingly authentic.

To contact Tony Parsons or to find out additional information about his talks, workshops, and retreats, please write or e-mail:

HDTV
Cranborne, Dorset
BH21 5PZ
ENGLAND

E-mail: theconnections@btinternet.com
Website· www.theopensecret.com

INNERDIRECTIONS PUBLISHING is the imprint of the Inner Directions Foundation—a nonprofit, educational organization dedicated to exploring authentic pathways to awakening to one's essential nature, in the spirit of Self-inquiry.

Our activities include publication of the highly acclaimed *Inner Directions Journal* and a distinctive selection of book, video, and audio titles that reflect clear and direct approaches to realizing *That* which is eternal and infinite within us.

These publications reflect the nondualistic "ground" from which religions and spiritual traditions arise—the infinite consciousness that lies at the Heart of all.

To request information or a free catalog of publications call, write, or e-mail:

INNER DIRECTIONS
P.O. Box 130070
Carlsbad, CA 92013

Tel: (760) 599-4075
Fax: (760) 599-4076
Orders: (800) 545-9118

E-mail: mail@InnerDirections.org
Website: www.InnerDirections.org